INSTRUCTIONS
TO THE
YOUNG BOOKSELLER

OLEANDER PRESS

Oleander Press
16 Orchard Street
Cambridge
CB1 1JT
www.oleanderpress.com

A CIP catalogue record for the book is available from the British Library.

ISBN: 9780900891960

Cover image reproduced with the kind permission of Triss Driver.

Designed and typeset by Ayshea Carter. manganese@ntlworld.com

INSTRUCTIONS
TO THE
YOUNG BOOKSELLER

OLEANDER PRESS

CONTENTS

FOREWORD

In these early years of the twenty-first century, traditional bookselling is being challenged from all sides by new and sophisticated competitors, both terrestrial and virtual. The book itself is even being re-imagined and reconfigured as data on a screen.

Such technical wizardry was undreamt of when the talk to young booksellers that you are holding was delivered. We believe it was given by Ernest W. Heffer, Chairman of the company until 1948, delivered in 1933 to a gathering of apprentices in London.

Although we believe we know the date of its delivery, its content would largely have been applicable to booksellers at any time between 1900 and about 1990 when computerised inventories first appeared. The basic principles it describes - be tidy, accurate, well read, up to date with events and respond to your customers' needs - still hold true for booksellers today.

It is surely cause for celebration that, although a lot has changed, much of what made bookselling special at the time still makes it so today.

However, for all its amusing anachronism, this brief book also holds more than a hint of melancholy for those of us employed in the traditional book trade. Much as our loyal customers still want and demand the benefits of a 'proper' bookshop, we are all aware that the future for most bookshops is a challenging one.

Whilst that is undeniable, it remains ever more true that those of us who feel that singular excitement, that Christmas-morning thrill, every time we enter our favourite bookshop, will continue to cherish them. It behoves us to pass on that passion to the next generation.

As Ernest says 'a bookshop is a microcosm of everything of importance that is happening in the world'. We certainly hope that this is as true of Heffers today as it was all those years ago.

David Robinson
Manager, Heffers Booksellers

INTRODUCTION

B EFORE I COMMENCE my talk, let me make it clear that it is addressed exclusively to young people working in bookshops. I understand that a number of you are not so engaged, and I fear that what I have to say will, if it does not bore, seem tedious and perhaps unhelpful to those. But as you are all in one way or another connected with the craft of books, I hope that all may be able to gather up some crumbs of interest from what must naturally be specialised, and therefore somewhat stodgy, fare. If one man's meat is another man's poison, then some of you are likely to be in a sad way by the time I have finished.

I am to talk to you about the training of the bookseller, but before I do so, will you let me tell you what I consider are the necessary qualifications of everyone who aspires to become a bookseller? In the first place, he or she (and there is no doubt that we men, sooner or later, will have to reckon with the competition of women) must possess a good memory for titles. I know that a memory can be improved, but if there is no memory to begin with, then not even a lifelong association with books will make it a good one. Next, I would insist upon the candidate being able to speak the mother tongue reasonably correctly; be sufficiently educated to the extent of being capable of reading, with a fair measure of accuracy, titles of books which might be considered difficult; and finally, he or she should be able to write a letter more or less grammatically correct, and in a legible hand. Now, as I know all of you will easily pass this test, I will proceed.

I propose to take a typical day's work, and examine and comment on its varied detail from the opening to the closing of the shop. This will enable us to get down to practical things at once and should suggest the kind of mental output which a bookseller should possess.

I should like you to have your notebooks before you, so that you may make a note of anything which I may not have made clear, or upon which you do not agree with me: I expect there will be a great deal. And then, at the end of the talk, we will discuss these obscurities and differences, and endeavour to arrive at a mutual understanding, so that you may go home without any befogging cobwebs in your brain, and I back to Cambridge a more practical and, I hope, a wiser and possibly humbler man, as the result of being attacked by the future booksellers of London.

THE OPENING OF THE SHOP

Preparatory steps and the vivid personalities of pipes

I WILL ASSUME THAT the shop opens at nine, and that all the staff is ready for the opening. Now let us definitely understand each other about this. It is obvious that if the shop is to open, there must be assistants to open it. The books may be willing to be sold, but they cannot sell themselves. So let me urge you, with all the emphasis of which I am capable, to make punctuality one of the keynotes of your life. The unpunctual being – man or woman – is a source of unending vexation to the community. It is a form of indolence and causes immense inconvenience to everybody with whom they are brought into contact. The assistant who is habitually three minutes late is a three-minutes-below-par man; he suffers, at first consciously, and later unconsciously, three minutes worth of mental trouble every time he is late. He knows it is wrong: he knows it is not fair to his employer nor fair to the other assistants. But so engrained does the habit become that it seems to sap his moral fibre, and he allows it to tyrannise over him, and to make him constantly uncomfortable, and to the end of his days he just steps in three minutes late.

But we must get back to our shop. The clock is striking nine: the blinds are being drawn up, and the door is open, and some of you will be there. If all of you were there, I should be able to say that you had all had a cold tub and were thoroughly well-groomed from head to toe. Hair will be brushed and oiled, though of course not over done, according to the latest fashion. Hands will be clean and nails duly manicured – they will not make themselves aggressive by showing traces of what they had been doing in either the immediate present or the remote past; and of course none of the fingers will show evidence of having been tinted a yellow hue not designed by nature. Cigarette smoke I understand is sometimes responsible for this. A bookseller is brought into such close relationship with his customers that he cannot be too particular about his personal appearance. I would even suggest that if a pipe is smoked it is knocked out a few minutes before entering the shop. Some pipes have a very vivid personality.

Different shops will, of course, have different methods. Some will have dust-sheets hung up at night to protect the books from that most pestiferous person, the dirty sweeper. Others, and those perhaps the majority, will leave the books to the mercy of the merciless, and so the duster and the dusting brush must be actively employed. We will assume that our bookshop has no dust-sheets and that Mr Sweeper, when practising his profession, thought only about getting the job done, and not of the best method of doing it. The books, therefore, will bear rich evidence of his handiwork, and it will be your task to eradicate that.

There is a great art in dusting, and speaking in general terms, men are not adept at the art. They regard it as something to be got over as soon as possible: they look upon it as something beneath them, and possibly would rather tolerate the dirt, than make the necessary effort to remove it. Should there be any traces of such nonsense dawdling about any of you, then get rid of it, I implore you. Learn to dust, and learn to do it properly. Don't crumple the duster in your hand, as if in fear that your friend, if he or she were passing at the time, might see you in the act of dusting. There is nothing to be ashamed of; and in time you will grow to consider the duster one of your most valuable tools. Don't slash it about, and don't just flick the dusting brush about. Dust, like Newton's apple, is subject to the laws of gravity; and if you just disperse it into the air, remember that it has to come down again, if not upon your particular lot of books, then upon those under the care of your fellow apprentices, and, as you know, the other man's dirt is an abomination. Let your motto be: 'Dust thoroughly, but tidily, and with method'.

Presumably, you will have a definite part of the shop allotted to you to keep clean: so each morning you will first do the superficial dusting – the tables, ledges and so on, and then you systematically go through the shelves, doing a certain amount each day. Remember to begin at the top, and work downwards. Dusting serves a very important double purpose; primarily it keeps the books clean: but there is another use equally important: it enables you to get familiar with the books, to check the alphabetical order, to see that all stock is represented, and generally to put shipshape what had been disarranged yesterday during the previous day's business. One word of caution. If the books are dirty, it may be necessary to bank them: do this carefully, so that the jackets may not be damaged: don't take more volumes than you can easily hold in your hands, and see that the books are really in order when you replace them. If a set of books has been moved, cast your eyes over the volumes to see that all are there, and are consecutive. Let the books be absolutely flush with the front of the shelves. This can be done by placing them loosely on, and slightly projecting from, the shelves in the first instance, and then drawing the palm of your hand across them, using the shelf as a guide. A section of books properly finished in this manner has a splendidly dignified appearance. Try to avoid having books lying on the tops of other books: it gives the shelves a most untidy appearance, and often it deters lazy people, who may be browsing around, from drawing out the books under them.

As juniors, you will probably be called upon to do considerably more dusting and cleaning than the other assistants. Take this as a right and cheerful duty, but don't do it mechanically: learn something from it as you do it. You might, and probably would be lectured if you were to commence reading and then neglect your work; but without actually reading the books, you can take notice of their titles, and if occasionally a title inspires you to look inside, then no one will say you 'nay'. It is the constant browsing and peeping – proving it is done intelligently – which makes a bookseller. To keep the body fit we all indulge in frequent bouts of eating, and if a bookseller is to make his mind fit, then he must read and read, and after that – read.

Presumably while you have been dusting the assistants have been busy dressing the windows, replacing from stock books sold the previous day, and attending to customers. The rule of this particular shop is that apprentices do not serve unless actually called upon to do so by an assistant. There is, however, no reason why you should not quietly listen to what is going on. This is the all-inspiring charm of a bookshop, when there are customers about: there is always something to listen to. Let me advise you then to learn to listen, and gradually you will find that you listen to learn.

There is nothing more fascinating than listening to a well-informed assistant talking about books to an educated customer. I don't mean that garrulous and empty talk about the number of copies being sold of any particular book, or the latest 'hit' and so on; but knowing or having grasped his customer's taste, he produces books likely to appeal, quoting reviews, giving the opinions he has received from other customers, showing contents-pages, pointing out illustrations, drawing attention to certain paragraphs in the books, and in return he receives – what an assistant prizes above all else – the customer's own opinion of the books; and if, as it may well be, the customer is one possessing authority, then the bookshop becomes almost a university, and only a fool would fail to learn. So let me repeat, learn to listen, that you may listen to learn.

LOOKING OUT THE ORDERS

*General best practices and
accounting for the Mrs Joneses' 1/6d*

T HE DAY IS DEVELOPING: the post has been opened by those responsible, and the orders have to be looked out, and I will assume that you have so far progressed as to be entrusted with the looking out of some of those orders. But before you begin, see that the section you were dusting is properly in order, and that there are no odd books straying about. First note that each order has been stamped by a rubber stamp before being handed to you.

That stamp in all probability will give the date the order was received, and the department or assistant it has to be passed to. There will be space in which to record when the order was executed, and, if money has been sent with the order, this will also be clearly indicated.

Perhaps to some of you my suggested method will appear unusual: to others it may seem useless. To the former, I would say that a different method really doesn't matter, for we are all aiming at efficiency, trying to eliminate mistakes, trying to avoid delay. To the latter, I would suggest that they weigh method against method, and judge which is the better of the two.

Now let us consider the various points in the stamp. The meaning of the date is obvious - it is, as it were, the starting point of the order, and it is up to you as a cog in the machinery of the shop to see how rapidly you can get it to the winning post which is the date of execution. The reason for indicating the department or assistant to which it has been passed will also be obvious. Should any question arise as to who was responsible for its execution, the fact will be given on the order itself, and praise or blame can be meted out. It isn't always the bookseller who is at fault when a delay has occurred in the execution of an order; frequently, when a customer has grumbled that an order he sent a fortnight ago has not been attended to – why? – upon referring to the order it will be found that there has been no delay. True it is dated a fortnight ago, but it was only received two days ago, as your stamp bears witness. So in all probability someone has carried it in his pocket – it couldn't have been 'her' pocket, because ladies have no pockets – and simply forgotten to post it. Method has saved you, you see; and a letter can be sent to the indignant lady or gentleman, regretting the delay but pointing out that you, at any rate, are not responsible for it.

The next point in the stamp to be considered is the indication of the receipt of money with the order. Now I want you to consider this point very carefully with me, for it is a most important one, and one which can be very fruitful of trouble. It will be admitted, I am sure, by every responsible person, that it would be unwise just to pin the money on to the order, as it was passed into the shop: it might get lost, for money can get lost; it might be mislaid, and it might even be stolen. Money can be sent in so many different forms – by cheque, money or postal order, by stamps, or even by actual cash; and to have this just floating about is only to invite trouble. It is therefore advisable that all monies sent with orders should be retained by the office or counting house, and the amount received clearly indicated on the order when it is opened. The order will then be looked up, and charged, and the bill will be presented to the office, and the amount sent by the customer will be claimed by the assistant, or by someone deputed to do so. Now, if the business is a large one, there must clearly be some straightforward method by which the amount in question can be identified by the office. To ask for Mrs Jones's 1/6d, if there have been a lot of payments, is going to cause a lot of searching and possibly confusion. It might easily be that two Mrs Jones sent 1/6d; and if the office has no means of identifying one from the other, and should the second Mrs Jones's order be mislaid, then the office could only pay out the 1/6d demanded and hope for the best about the second 1/6d. But suppose that the order was numbered, and the office had receptacles – bags, envelopes, or something of the kind – corresponding with those numbers – in which the money could be placed; and if in addition, it had a book which was correspondingly numbered, with a space for the name, and space in which to place the date showing when the money was paid out, and another space in which the department or assistant's name responsible for handling the order was shown; and finally a cash column which stated the amount received: then the complete record of the whole transaction would be available: and should it be impossible to execute the order, the money could be returned without appearing both as a payment and paid out in the cash takings of the day. The cash record book will be scrutinized each day by the cashier, and any monies not claimed by departments can be enquired about.

This all may sound a little formidable: but really it is extremely simple in actual working. If I had to describe to you the best method of cleaning your boots, I am quite sure you would decide that the thing was so complicated that you would prefer to have dirty boots, rather than work to such an elaborate formula.

I may have laboured this point overmuch, but I have done so quite deliberately; because it is only by attending to small points that the business can be made to run smoothly. Please a new customer by your promptitude, and in all probability you will have made a permanent customer.

Now let us look at one of the orders. Glance at the address: it may be that it is written from New Zealand or Japan, or some other end of the earth. The possibilities of this are one of the great attractions of a bookseller's shop. The post knows no limit, and except from a time point of view, a bookseller is only the nearest post-box distance from the most distant book buyer. This privilege, and it is a great privilege, should ever be in the mind of a book-seller – his potential customers reach to the ends of the earth. If the thought of this does not make you young people proud, then all I can say is, that I know of nothing which will.

But if it is a privilege, it is also a responsibility. A mistake on your part in reading the letter or the instructions may possibly cause a six months delay – and it is not thus that customers are either made or kept. So read the order carefully right through. The office will have checked whether the writer has an account, or is entitled to credit; or possibly you may be instructed by the office to send a pro-forma, or to despatch by

C.O.D. Possibly all money details will be attended to by the charging and invoicing clerk; but you should have this very important point always well in your mind. It is very easy to sell books to certain people: but if those people do not intend to, or even intend to, but do not, pay for them, then the transaction is no longer a sale, but a gift: and gifts of this nature do not make balance sheets, or rather, they make adverse ones.

Before any books are looked out, then, be sure that the person ordering is entitled to have them. We will assume that the order is O.K'd by the office, and that it has to be looked out. Now is your chance to show that you have profited by your previous experiences. The honour of your shop is for the moment in your hands, and, believe me, it is so easy to stain that honour. A little want of thought, or care, and the thing is done. Obviously, I cannot take you through a mass of orders, and point out the pitfalls which surround each. I can only generalise. Read the whole letter through first, and carefully note if there are any special forwarding instructions. The books ordered may be intended as a present for a friend of the customer. Don't send the books to Nigeria when you should send them to Croydon. Such a thing has been done, and great annoyance given. Get clearly into your mind what your customer wants: don't jump to conclusions. If everything is not absolutely clear, consult those above you. The field is so vast that no single brain can grasp it all; but there are older assistants at hand whose experience is wider and whose knowledge is deeper than yours. So let another motto be your guide: when in doubt, ask. There is no stigma attached to one who has to ask, rather it should be regarded as a sign of efficiency. Don't ask stupid and irritating questions; don't ask when a reference to a catalogue would make the matter clear. But when your knowledge and your imagination have failed to solve the problem, and when the catalogues don't seem to help you – then ask, and you will find help readily and generously given.

The next thing to be sure about is that you are sending the customer exactly what he asks for. The whole order may be for one shilling book: but that shilling book was really wanted: otherwise the customer would not have taken the trouble to write for it – it may be from five thousand miles away. If he asks for a text of Caesar, see that he gets it, and not a text of Julius Caesar. Try to imagine yourself the customer, and think what you would say or should not say if, after waiting three months, you received Weldon's "Knitting" instead of Welldon's "Netting". These are by no means impossible mistakes: they are very possible ones, and do occur with irritating frequency.

Each establishment will have its own method of charging; be loyal to that method, because by doing so you will avoid both mistakes and losses. In the best-regulated shops mistakes do occur, and books have been sent off without being charged; but such transactions do not very materially help to swell the returns of your department. I ask you, therefore, zealously to respect the general instructions of your shop. We are all anxious to become efficient, and efficiency can only be achieved by method.

I will assume that those orders which you can execute from stock are passed on to the despatch department, and for the moment we will leave them to be charged; later on, we will see how they are charged and sent off.

But what about those orders which cannot be executed from stock? Here is the testing-ground for the merits of a bookshop. What is going to happen to the little odd-and-end order – the request for a twopenny tract, for a shilling hymn-book – the sort of thing which is not and need not be in stock? The things which are profitless and seem so little worthwhile. How are these to be dealt with? For the moment they do not concern us: you doubtless will pass them on to the order department, and hope for the best: but later on they too must concern us – so be prepared.

NEW STOCK RECEIPTS

including the important distinction between labelling and Mabelling

THE SHOP IS NOW filling up with customers, and we will presume that you are no longer wanted there, and have been instructed to go and assist the receiving department, and help to check and mark off the books which have come from the publishers.

Now be alert here, for in proportion as you memorise the new books as they come in, so will your bookselling knowledge progress. Don't get mechanical: suggest to yourself that all these books have to be remembered: the titles, prices, sizes, general appearance, and publishers; and if the suggestion is really meant and believed in, you will remember. This is the all-wonderful thing about a bookseller's brain – its capacity for storing a vast mass of unrelated facts, and its power to give those facts out again as they are wanted. But remember, if you allow yourself and your brain to become mechanical, you may handle a book a hundred times and promptly forget it a hundred times. Acquire in the first instance the habit of remembering by conscious effort, and in time you will find that you remember unconsciously.

I will assume that there are two doing this particular job; one will take the invoice, and the other look out and mark the books as they are called out. One word of warning. Never, never pass into stock books for which you have no invoice. To do so is only to ask for future trouble. The invoices may have been lost, and should you pass the books, relying on your memory to see that the invoice does eventually come, and suppose that it does not, and suppose that your memory plays you false, what is going to happen when the publishers' statement comes in? The invoice clerk will interview you, and trouble has been known to result.

Let me counsel you in this as in all business matters to treat what you are doing seriously. I know that last night's dance, when Mabel slipped down and pulled you with her, was a most momentous affair; but it does not belong to your business life. So keep the two things quite distinct. The present job is to check and mark off the books before you. Concentrate on that – Mabelling can come after the shop is closed.

As the items of the invoice are read out, see that the books really tally. The vast majority of books today have the price printed on their jackets, so that checking is quite simple. But don't let its simplicity lull you into slackness. Publishers' clerks have been known to make mistakes both against their firm and against the booksellers, so be watchful, and bring any mistakes at once to the notice of those who are responsible for clearing them up. I need hardly mention that any mistakes the publishers may make against themselves will be treated with the same care for correction as mistakes the other way. It is only by this standard of honour in small as well as big things that a business is carried to success. In all probability you will not be called upon to check the extensions; but for your own edification it is worth doing. It will make you conversant with the various terms of the publishers, and incidentally give you a little mental arithmetic.

Despite the large number of jacketed books, there are still some which will require marking. See that this is done neatly and lightly: there is nothing which offends more than ugly, sprawling figures. When you see your chum licking his pencil preparatory to marking a book, just gently put your hand on his shoulder and tell him that lead is bad for the complexion, and licking bad for the pencil and worse for the books.

When all the books are marked off, you will presumably inform the order department of the fact, and then doubtless someone responsible will see that the publishers have sent neither more nor less than was ordered. If more have been sent, it will at once be questioned why; if less, the reason must be ascertained. There is a very important point to be noted here. Should an invoice state that certain books are reprinting, binding, or out of print, attention should be called to the facts; otherwise, and particularly if the books are wanted for an order, delay may result.

Let us assume that on this occasion everything is correct. What is now to happen to the books? In the first instance those books which are wanted for definite orders will be sorted out, and be sent to the despatch department; the remainder will be divided into two piles, one being those books which have been ordered to replace sold stock, and the other new publications. We will see how both of these piles are disposed of. The former is taken into the shop, divided into subjects, and worked away into their sections in the shelves. Those shops which have tied stock will put what they can on the shelves and tie up the rest, putting them into what too often may be called the cemetery. For unless there is a very rigorous method of checking sales, the tied stock may easily be forgotten, and a book, of which there is tied stock, be reported as, "Sorry we have just sold the last copy – may we order for you?" Either every book sold must be recorded somewhere, or there must be evidence of some sort in the books on the open shelves to show that there is tied stock. I favour the latter method. A labelling card of distinctive colour, giving details of tied stock, and placed in one of the copies on the shelves and turned over the top of the book, so that it is quite obvious, is a very workable arrangement, provided that the assistants will treat these cards as really valuable documents. Any assistant who sells a book with one of those cards in is to be regarded with as much abhorrence as the man who removes his neighbour's landmark.

As for the books on the other pile, what is going to happen to them? I hope that every book is going to be looked at by every assistant, and I hope that each one will say to himself, "Now who will be interested in this?" We are now in the very crucible of bookselling; are we coming out as refined gold, or merely desultory dross?

Each of these new publications represents a very considerable capital sum expended by the publishers on producing what presumably they believe to be a good and wanted book; and they rely to a great extent on we booksellers to do our best to make the book known; and in proportion as we respond to that reliance, so is our bookselling reputation enhanced, both with the book buying public and, which is of equal moment, with the publishers.

If these new books are just placed with the other new books, and left to the mercy of the winds and weathers of publishers' advertising departments alone, we will soon come to the regrettable situation where one could say we deserve the reproach which once was hurled at me, that 'any fool can sell a book'. But if we are going to take some trouble to make these books known, by sending out prospectuses, and posting titles, by writing special letters or by persistent introduction in the shop; then, but not till then, shall we be worthy of the name of booksellers, and worthy of our hire in the shape of better terms from the publishers.

THE DESPATCH DEPARTMENT

Avoiding the menace, seeding the wayside,
and confirmation of two and two

W E WILL NOW GO TO the despatch
department, and see what is happening to those
books which have been ordered, some of which
you looked out, and others were taken from the books received
from the publishers which you have just marked off.

There are many methods of dealing with the daily
orders received: some are over-elaborate and others madly
slovenly. In the particular shop we are working in, an

intermediate method has been adopted. When the orders are received, they are at once passed out to the head assistant who, in turn, hands them on to juniors to look out the books which are in stock: you will remember that we have already helped in this. When they are completed as far as possible, they are passed back to the order department, where the books not in stock are procured by the collectors from the publishers. London methods naturally differ from country methods, and as I am talking to Londoners, I will look at things from that point of view. The collectors, in due course, will bring the books to the receiving department, the ritual of which we have just been through, and the books are before us. Again, methods will vary with each establishment: but speaking in general terms, if the number of books ordered is considerable, it will facilitate the finding of them as they are received if they are arranged in alphabetical order. In the first instance, the current orders will be dealt with. Those which for some reason or another cannot be executed will be placed on one side, to be attended to later. The completed orders will be passed to the charging clerk, who will charge on duplicate and numbered invoices, one to go to the customer, the other to be retained. By this method the clumsy and laborious Day Book is entirely eliminated – the duplicate invoice taking its place. It will at once be recognised that these invoices are to be treated with scrupulous care, because if they become lost, or are mislaid, all record of the transaction will have vanished, and the amount of such invoices become a charge upon the profits.

After the current day's orders have been attended to, the next consideration will be those previous orders which for some reason or another have not been executed. These orders will have been filed in alphabetical order, so that any query can at once be answered. Now, a satisfied customer is a great asset to a firm; but a dissatisfied one is or can be a positive menace; which is but another way of saying, see that every order receives proper and intelligent attention, and, above and beyond all, see that an early intimation is given to the customer of any books that cannot be sent. Let the reply be as specific and definite as possible. It is to this end I cautioned you to take particular note of any remarks on the publishers' invoices. O/P or R/P are easily overlooked; but in both cases they mean that some book or books are not going to be sent; and if you forget, or overlook to advise your customer, you know perfectly well that in the course of a post or two a brusque letter will come; and you will be told that if you cannot execute orders promptly, he or she will find someone who will.

To avoid constantly handling orders which it is definitely known cannot be executed for some time, it is advisable to place all such in a separate file, or enter in an abeyance book, which should be very frequently gone through, so that nothing may be overlooked.

After all orders have been looked out, and charged,

labels will be typed, and in spaces specially provided, the number of volumes in the parcel, together with the invoice number, will be given. This enables the packer to check his work, and easily to refer in case of discrepancy. The books are now ready for the packing room; but one moment, please: before they are sent down, insert a prospectus or two: it may, of course, be seed sown on the wayside, but perchance it may fall on fertile soil, and orders result; so make it the rule of your life – in packing a book, always include a prospectus.

Let us visit the packing room and see what happens there. The books we have just seen charged have just been received, and are being packed. The labels are read first to see if the books are for home or abroad: if parcel or book-post, passenger or goods train. They are then carefully packed, and a great deal of the customer's pleasure or displeasure depends on this. Each packet is then recorded in its particular post or rail book, and, as far as we are concerned, the transaction is finished – unless by chance we have done our work badly, and a reproachful letter follows; or, as we should hope or be sure that if anything comes it will be a letter of commendation; and such letters are much more likely to result in your progress than are reproachful ones.

The office arrangements and procedure hardly come within the scope of this essay. As a rule a special clerical staff is responsible for what goes on; but I strongly advise everyone to have an acquaintance with the outlines of bookkeeping: it is an admirable tonic for the intellect, and enables you to see, and to prove, that two added to two, in whatever form they present themselves, always make four; and, after all, this is the chief thing which bookkeeping demonstrates.

ATTENDING THE CUSTOMER

Psychoanalysis and Humpty Dumpty

L ET US NOW GET BACK to the shop and see what is happening there. Judging from the number of people looking at the windows, there must be something exciting within. Did the assistant responsible for their arrangement make an unusual display when he dressed them this morning? Let us look together. No. There is nothing unusual, but the assistant knew his job. Notice how he has put the topical books in prominent positions. Subjects which are being discussed in the papers, books which are being well and extensively reviewed and advertised, books which have a special seasonal appeal; all are there; and that is why so many people are attracted. This is what every good bookshop should do. In the first place, the windows should be scrupulously clean and attractive, and, secondly, they should be topical and up to date. Study these points: mentally arrange the windows yourselves, because in time it may be your job to be responsible for the window display; and much can be learned by observation both of your own and also the shop window of other shops.

Now for our final and greatest experience: I mean, of course, the attending to our customers' wants. I should like in the first instance to give you two or three golden rules to remember. If a customer expresses a wish, or appears to want to browse round, let him; this is where a bookshop differs from almost every other kind of shop. The motto for other businesses is, don't keep customers waiting, but in our shops the rule should be, do not be unduly anxious to serve, unless your customer shows an evident desire to be attended to. For the younger assistant I would advocate an attitude midway between assertiveness and timidity; and in the case of a customer who seems to possess authority, I would recommend that he be left to the care of a more experienced assistant. If you are asked for a book, the title of which you have never heard of, don't conclude you haven't got it, and say so; and, above all, don't try to bluff and talk through your hat: for in all probability your customer knows forty times more about the subject than you do, and although he may not call you fool to your face, he may think it, and he will say it to someone; and not only you, but your shop, will suffer in reputation. Be respectful at all times and to everybody.

Let us now ask that young man who is waiting to be attended to what he requires. "Are you being attended to, Sir?" "No. Have you got a book on Psychoanalysis?" Now, I am sure there is no one in this room who has not heard of Psychoanalysis, so the request is a perfectly natural one. What is the procedure? You will take your customer to the section where Psychology is shelved. I have elsewhere given my views on classification, and I can only say here that I hope that the classification of your shop is of a logical nature. Psychology should be somewhere near Philosophy, so with a full confidence we can go there, and if you know nothing about the books, point out where they are on the shelves, and go and get expert help. If, however, you are sure of your knowledge, show the books you have, and give your reasons for recommending the particular book you do. If you find yourself baffled by a question, don't lightly hand on the difficulty to another, but make a mental note of the query and turn up an Encyclopaedia or a Dictionary, and the next time the question is put to you, you will be competent to answer it yourself. There is one thing you may be perfectly certain of, and that one thing is the joy and attraction of all true bookshops. It is this, that however long you remain a bookseller, and however keen you may be in trying to master all there is to know, there will still be an infinity of things and books you won't know; so always let your confidence be tempered by caution: otherwise like Humpty Dumpty you will constantly be having bad falls.

I am going to assume that you were successful in selling a book, and that you have requested to enter it, as the young man has an account with your firm. If you are certain on this point, make out the necessary invoice, taking care to get the name, address, and title of the book correct, and put the top copy with the book. Never allow a customer to leave before this is done. Books can so easily be given away. Next, you will do up the book neatly, after first putting a prospectus or advertisement in the parcel. This is a very rough and ready treatment of a very complex process, but I think it may be regarded as fairly typical, and I can leave it to you to apply it to the thousand and one possibilities of a bookshop routine.

THE END OF THE DAY

The Microcosm, the Dodo and the Dance

WE ARE GETTING TO the end of our subject, and also to the end of our day; but there is one department I must take you to before I leave you, and that is the letter-filing department. There are, of course, many methods of filing – what the method is, does not matter much: all that is necessary is that every letter and order received, and a copy of every letter sent, should be easily accessible. The old wire file is, I hope, as dead as the dodo. In the present department, as you will notice, the original letter, together with any reply, is filed away in cabinets in strict alphabetical order, and only the clerk responsible for the filing is allowed to touch those cabinets. On the efficiency with which the work is done, rests the peace of mind of half the establishment.

Well, it is nearly closing-time. Throughout the whole shop all vital documents and valuables will be placed in the strong-room, the assistants will generally tidy up the shop, and leave their desks so that should they be prevented from coming tomorrow, there won't be muddle and turmoil for someone else to clear up. Respect the closing hour as you respect the opening one, except that if there is something of importance to be finished, see that it is done, and done not grudgingly, but with real enthusiasm; for as the business prospers as the result of loyal cooperation on the part of all the workers, so will the reward prosper: it is for such legitimate prosperity we all work.

The working day is finished, and you may be off to your dance or the cinema or to whatever amusement attracts you; but for the great cause of bookselling, add, I beseech you, a definite course of reading – not the snippety and pernicious reading of short stories, nor the peptonised form of literature provided by many of the so-called literary papers: acquire the habit of reading the more serious and solid book, for by so doing you will provide yourself with a hobby which will last you all through life, and by that hobby you will be moulding yourself for your high calling.

Read the reviews of books which appear in the important literary papers – the Times Literary Supplement should loom large in your life; read the trade papers so that you may be familiar with everything which is going on in the world of books.

And as a bookshop is a microcosm of everything of importance which is happening in the world, because sooner or later, whatever the subject, be assured that a book will be written on it, it is the duty of the bookseller to keep himself abreast of current things in every field of life; and as he is expected to know of all past things, it seems as though the Encyclopaedia Britannica ought to be his constant reading; but after the first few volumes this tends to be a little dull and heavy.

Does all this sound rather fearsome and heavy going? I have purposely caricatured things somewhat, but there is a large element of truth in what I have said. A bookseller, if he is to be worthy of the name, must be widely read, and if our bookshops in the future are to be what bookshops should be, then it is to you we should look. Equip yourselves for the greatest of all adventures – for this is what bookselling really is – and you will receive a double reward: the satisfaction of having done your part by way of personal service to the community to the best of your ability, and that equally important satisfaction of reaping a greater material reward for your services.